Meditation

The Benefits Of Meditation And Mindfulness Practices For Achieving True Contentment And Awakening

(Techniques Of Easy Meditation Suitable For Novices To Help Reduce Stress And Anxiety And Improve Sense Of Well-being Right Away)

Alvin Hamelin

TABLE OF CONTENT

Your Guide To Bringing More Love And Happiness Into Your Life 1

Today Is The Day When I Have To Make The Purchase. 6

A Dissection Of The Human Condition 16

MEDITATION USING THE DIVINE VERB 18

The Beginnings Of A Meditation Practice 23

Meditation Techniques 30

What Exactly Does It Mean When Someone Says They Are Mindful, And In What Ways May It Benefit You? 36

Getting Back In Touch With Your Developing Intuition 50

How Are You Supposed To Read This Book? 70

Mantra Meditation 90

Meditation With Clare Is An Easy-To-Follow Guided Practice Perfect For Novices And Busy People. 93

The Practice Of Getting Ready To Meditate 101

Mindfulness Is About Much More Than Just Stress Relief 115

Getting Started With Meditation — The Actual Practice 120

What Exactly Are The Advantages Of Meditating Creatively? 131

Your Guide To Bringing More Love And Happiness Into Your Life

Meditation is one method to love yourself, which is the first step towards attracting love and happiness into your life. The first step is to love yourself first, and one way to love yourself is to meditate every day. Daily meditations provide you the opportunity to put yourself, the most important person in your life, at the forefront of your attention. When you give yourself space to collect your thoughts and feelings, you begin to develop a deeper appreciation for who you are. And at that point, you'll understand that individuals who love themselves first are inherently more deserving of all the wonderful things that come their way.

You offer yourself the chance to bask in fresh energy when you let go of negative ideas and allow yourself to move on. Meditation and introspection are fantastic techniques to revitalize your energies and get a better handle on your thoughts since they give you more of a sense of agency. Because what you think about ultimately determines how you conduct your life, you must begin with your thoughts if you want to bring love and happiness into your life in order to be successful.

A life guided by purpose

You'll figure out how to provide meaning to your life if you meditate on a consistent basis. Discovering your life's genuine calling is something that can only be done when there is no noise around you. It's possible that life will become more loud than you'd want it to be at times. It doesn't take much carelessness to realize that one has been disoriented among all of the activity going on around them. When you sit quietly in meditation, you will, at long last, become aware of the things that make your heart sing. Permit yourself to get completely immersed in the experience at hand since it is precisely at this time that you will have a true understanding of your true identity.

Maintain your sincerity.

Meditation not only teaches you to be honest with the people around you, but it teaches you to be honest with yourself as well. Ask yourself now, what are the falsehoods that you have been telling yourself on a regular basis? Do you have a habit of telling yourself that you aren't deserving of happiness or that you don't deserve to be loved by others? If you often subject yourself to depressing ideas, you are not only doing damage to your sense of who you are as a person, but you are also setting the stage for a cycle of misery in your life. When you give falsehoods permission to run your life, you sabotage every opportunity you have of being loved and experiencing happiness in your life. You will be able to examine your thoughts and distinguish between the truth and falsehoods when you meditate. There is nothing to be embarrassed of when you allow honesty to enter your life.

Explore new places and try out new things.

Meditation is beneficial for a number of reasons, one of which is that it widens your mind and makes it more open to the possibility of searching out new experiences. As your mental capacity increases, you will naturally develop a heightened awareness of the world around you. People, places, and events that were once unimportant to you are now taking on new significance for you. There is nothing that stimulates the mind quite like taking a little break from activity every now and then. When you meditate regularly, your mind will become more adept at taking in new knowledge with each subsequent session. This prepares you to accept significant shifts that are going to take place in your life in the near future.

When you live your life guided by a purpose, maintain honesty in everything that you do, and actively seek out new experiences, your life will become a magnet for all that is positive in the world. When you make meditation a regular part of your routine, love and happiness are sure to find their way to you sooner rather than later. If you want to live a life with greater significance, you should prioritize cultivating inner quiet. When you allow yourself time to be still and silent, you'll get a lot more insight into who you are as a person and how to interact with the environment that surrounds you.

Today Is The Day When I Have To Make The Purchase.

I was seated above them, and from that vantage point, I could see that they, too, were miserable. I said, "My cherished ones, could you please tell me about your difficulties?"

One of them added, "I am in desperate need of prestige."

I responded by saying, "Not a problem," and "Please take mine."

Someone another said, "I do not have any fame."

I responded by saying, "Not a problem," and "Please take mine."

Another person remarked, "I am in need of wealth."

I said, "Take all of my possessions," and they did.

One of them remarked, "I don't have enough education."

"Not a problem," I said, "please accept my degrees."

Another person chimed up, "I want to see the whole world."

"That's easy," I told her, "you can travel for me."

Someone another spoke in and said, "Master, I want power."

My response was, "No problem," and I said, "take what little I have."

One of them addressed the master and said, "Master, I need servants to help me carry out my responsibilities."

"You can have mine," I said in response.

Another person chimed in and added, "Master, I wish I could sit in such an elevated position."

"Oh! No problem; will you kindly take mine?

These things are pointless if the disciple does not have a direct relationship with the Lord in their heart, my loving disciples. You may all accumulate material goods, but what are the advantages of doing so? I want everyone of you to give me your desperation so that I may combine it with mine. If that happens, there is a chance that I will have enough money to buy a vision of the Lord dwelling inside my heart from the market for unadulterated devotional service.

The going rate is exorbitant, and I am not able to buy it on my own account because of this. Please assist me; I really need it. There is no worth in anything else. Give me your desperation because today I have to go out into the world and work for the Lord in the heart of people.

It is impossible for me to go back without Him.

Pose de Seiza

If you find that sitting in the Burmese posture is challenging or unpleasant for you in any manner, you may achieve more stability by kneeling on the floor and placing a cushion in between both of your legs.

Pose a la chaise

Try the simple chair posture if none of the poses described above work well for you. This is mostly due to the fact that it might be difficult for novices to hold the poses described above for even a few minutes at first. In this case, rather of working on a posture while seated on the ground, you will just need to sit on a chair. There is simply no need to be embarrassed about using a chair when one is required to do so. You are just beginning to practice meditation, and even if you weren't just beginning, but you felt like sitting on a chair while you meditate, you absolutely should do so.

Because meditation is a practice that does not prohibit you from doing what you desire to do or being who you choose to be, you should sit on a chair if you find that more comfortable. Only when you are able to relax comfortably will you be able to concentrate with the maximum attention. Take a seat in any chair that appeals to your sense of ease and allow yourself to relax there. Just make sure that you are not slouching and that both of your feet are firmly planted on the ground. Also, make sure that your knees and hips are aligned with your feet.

If you find that none of these postures work for you at first, you may always try meditating while lying down on the floor. The one and only drawback of sitting in a supine position while meditating is the high likelihood that you will become so calm and relaxed that you will fall asleep. If you want to practice meditation while lying down, place the exercise mat on the floor, support your knees up with a pillow, and place your feet flat on the ground. This instills a sensation of arousal inside you, allowing you to remain alert during the meditation exercise.

You are free to experiment with all of these positions one at a time before going on to the real practice in order to determine which one is most beneficial for you. Choose the one that makes you feel the most at ease, and then work on improving that skill. As soon as you feel comfortable in your current position, you should go to the second, third, and fourth points of the posture, respectively. These are discussed in further depth in the next chapter.

Confession Based on the Covenant

These are the words of a daughter-in-law to her mother-in-law, which Ruth says in the book of Ruth. They are typically uttered during weddings. These words are a powerful declaration of love, but they also mean so much more. It is a confession of faith made in the context of a covenant by a non-Jew. Ruth instructs Naomi to quit trying to convince her that they should go back to Moab. Why? The reason for this is because Ruth pledges that she will remain bound to Naomi regardless of the passage of time or distance. Ruth promises that she will follow Naomi wherever she goes and that she will set up camp in the same place as Naomi does. In this passage, Ruth makes a solemn oath to Naomi that no physical distance would ever come between them. In a similar fashion, Ruth says that she will pass away wherever Naomi passes away and that she will be buried wherever Naomi is buried. In this passage, Ruth makes a solemn oath to Naomi, assuring her that she would never leave Naomi's side, not even in death, when she is laid to rest next to her. This is the kind of love that won't let go no matter what.

Because to Ruth's selfless devotion, Naomi's people, who were included in the Abrahamic covenant as God's chosen people, will become her own, and Naomi's God will become her own. In this statement, the non-Jewish foreigner professes her belief in LORD, the living God of Israel, as well as her desire to join the Israelite congregation that is bound by the covenant. Ruth's heart has been won over by the grace of God in some way, shape, or form, and she has no choice but to join herself to him and his people. Because of this, she finds it impossible to give up on Naomi! The confidence that Ruth has in God compels her to love completely.

Ruth is being asked to pay a high price for her faith. It means saying goodbye to all that is comfortable in her life at this point. It means leaving her home for a faraway nation, her beloved family for some strangers who have had their circumcisions performed, her country of Moab for the land that was promised to Israel, and her deity Chemosh for Yahweh. This admission will have a profound impact on every aspect of Ruth's life. Her whole identity has undergone a dramatic transformation! She went from being a foreigner to the covenant promises of God and an outsider to the commonwealth of Israel to becoming a child of faith who is cherished by God (Ephesians 2:12-13)! For this reason, she is able to use the name of God's covenant in order to seal her confession of the covenant. Faith is necessary for following God, and faith inherently leads to doing extreme acts. To have faith is to forsake everything, even ourselves, and to seek for a new identity in the person of Jesus Christ. There is a significant financial cost associated with serving the God of Israel. However, if one chooses to ignore him, they will end up having to pay an even greater price.

A Dissection Of The Human Condition

The existence of humans is seen through a very limited lens. To us, being human means having both a physical and a mental component to our life. The mind is similar to a chaotic collection of ideas that are occuring in us. Other than our ideas, we do not have any other sense of what it means to exist psychologically.

There is a core breathing method in Kriya Yoga that is dependent on achieving a balance between the sun and moon energy currents that are found inside us. According to the sacred texts known as the Vedas, each of us has a vast network of energy centers that are referred to collectively as nadis. There are two primary nadis that are located inside of us. The solar plexus is one of them.It is often referred to as ida. The other is known as the lunar plexus.Pingala is the name given to this animal. The solar plexus is represented by the energy channel that flows through our right nostril. Moon current is the energy that flows from the left nostril, whereas solar current flows from the right. Following the practice of deep breathing in Kriya Yoga, both the solar and lunar plexus are brought into harmony, and there occurs an awakening of the shusumna nadi. There is stimulation of the shushumna nadi when the solar plexus and the lunar plexus are in harmony with one another. This encounter with that huge nadi inspires a profound sense of contentment and satisfaction inside each one of us. Wonderful things may come from attaining such a happy mood. We are living in a state of immense pleasure, joy, and bliss. Our minds get more expansive when we cultivate the discipline of profound meditation.

Ida and pingala are internal channels that function similarly to sympathetic and parasympathetic nervous system pathways. The world seems like a great place when you're in shushuman nadi.

Our broader intellect now has a significant amount of potential.

MEDITATION USING THE DIVINE VERB

Today we are going to teach a meditation that utilizes the divine verb. Although there are various words that we might use, we are going to pick Zmam Olamot.

This term refers to worshiping the Father via one's physical form as a method of entering parallel realms. Olamot are universes that exist in parallel to the actual world; they are the hidden gardens of Kabbalah.

Maintain complete stillness at a remote location, which may even be your own room as long as you shut the door and no one disturbs you while you're there. Maintain as much composure as you can with your breathing.

Take a deep breath in with your nose, and then let it out through your mouth.

Keep your eyes closed as you go through the steps again and again until you reach a state of extreme peace and relaxation.

When your mind is peaceful, breathe in through your nose and out through your mouth very gently. Repeat this many times. Pronounce the phrase "ZMAM OLAMOT" while you let out your breath.

In contrast to Devekut meditation, which focuses only on the mind and the thoughts it generates, pronounce while utilizing your voice.

When you let go of the air, as many times as you can while maintaining a very calm demeanor, repeat this expression.

During this process, you will start to have visions, and you will see them even more clearly when you are sleeping, in your dreams, and during other spiritual experiences. Your ability to see into the hidden world will improve throughout the day, and it will get much stronger at night.

You will establish a connection with the divine verb if you do this technique every day for ten minutes. One day you may use Kadosh Hashem, and the next day you can use Eloheno Melech Ha Olam. You have the ability to switch the divine word. It is essential that you maintain your meditation practice and keep a journal in which to record your experiences, since as time goes on, you will have a growing number of them.

Your spiritual development, learning from your inner awakening, but Rosh will explain you the meaning of the language used in the astral realm, is greatly aided by registering in a notebook and seeking assistance from a Rosh.

You are welcome to share your stories with me by email, where I will do my best to be of assistance. It is an email. Hashem will disclose vast secrets, secrets that pastors and priests will never be able to tell you because they are mortal like us, and the Creator, who is eternal, has great secrets from the cosmos to share with us. Hashem will reveal these secrets to us in the future.

Adonai has a desire to communicate his secrets to his servant prophets, just as he did in the past.

Hashem must reveal its secrets to humanity since nothing that has been created can remain static or immobile. The splendor of the father must grow, shedding light on our transitory soul and transforming it into something that is both eternal and strong.

Is the sun capable of remaining still without giving out any of its light or rays? Naturally, this is not feasible, since Hashem is much more powerful than we are, and because he wants to reveal his secrets, it is essential for us to only serve as vessels.

When we meditate, our minds transform into vessels that are intimately linked with the Being Who Created All of the Worlds.

When we have perfected our meditation practices, we merge into oneness with him.

Despite how swiftly the years and cycles pass, individuals who are in relationship with the Creator will endure eternally.

It is beneficial to take ten minutes out of each day to meditate since it not only helps the spirit but also has a positive effect on the physical body, providing health and well-being to the practitioner.

The physical body is strengthened, and avenues of connection with the soul that we all possess are opened, via the practice of meditation.

Praying, meditating, and abstaining from food are all excellent ways to allow the light of the Eternal to nurture the soul.

When we meditate, we are able to establish a connection with the universe's most fundamental source, which in turn nourishes us with unadulterated light—the light from which everything was born.

Through the practice of meditation, the barriers that separate the soul from the physical body are removed. This raises our vibration and gives rise to a new consciousness within us, one that enables us to perceive the spiritual battle that is taking place between light and chaos, as well as take part in this conflict and contribute to the evolution of both the universe and humanity.

The Beginnings Of A Meditation Practice

Do not rush into meditation just yet without first ensuring the following things have been taken care of:
You are responsible for cultivating an appropriate setting.
The location would be determined by two factors: the amount of room that is available and the sort of lifestyle that you lead. You should make sure that the location you choose for your meditation practice is serene, comfortable, and filled with natural light. You don't even need to have a really complex environment.

Just remember to make things as brief and basic as possible. Keep in mind that you are going to create your very own tranquil enclave in which to practice meditation. Do not feel disheartened if you are turned off by some noise from the outside that is beyond your control and that is contributing to your discomfort. With enough practice, you'll be able to put yourself into a meditative state regardless of where you are.

Find yourself a spot where you can relax. After you have found a place that is quiet and peaceful, the next thing you need to do is search for a seat that is comfortable. It is recommended that if you are going to sit on a chair, you go for one that has a firm back support. Armchairs are off limits since they have a propensity to make you feel comfortable and cause you to nod off. If you're going to sit on the floor, you may as well bring a mat or a towel with you. You may also find additional comfort by using a pillow. You may want to consider covering yourself in a cozy blanket if you are going to be seated for a significant amount of time.

It is very difficult to meditate if you are in an uncomfortable posture, and even the smallest noise will be enough to pull your attention away from the practice. In addition to this, you will find it difficult to sit motionless for any length of time.

A novice just has to sit for five minutes at a time to get significant benefits from meditation.

If you are just getting started with meditation, it is recommended that you sit quietly for at least five minutes at a time. It would not be advantageous to do it for a lengthy amount of time, particularly if you have just began the practice of meditation. Compare lengthy, infrequent sessions to shorter, more frequent ones. the latter are preferable. After a period of time, you may find that you are able to sit through longer sessions and develop a routine that is tailored to your needs.

A healthy way to get ready is to relax.

Before you start meditating, it is regarded a good ability to learn how to relax, since this will make each meditation session more successful for you. To begin, choose a comfortable sitting position, either on the floor or on a chair, and remain in that position until further instruction is given. Take a number of calm, deep breaths. Feel the relaxation in your muscles as you utter positive affirmations to yourself, such as "My muscles are relaxed," "My hands and arms are relaxing," "My mind is calm," "My body is calm," and "My mind is awake." Remember that keeping your mind and body calm may have a significant positive impact on your overall health. The body language of a person reveals very quickly whether or not they are calm.

Find the source of the physical tension.

In relation to being calm, it is also essential that you recognize any physical stresses that are mostly located in the back, neck, and shoulders. These regions of the body often hold all of the emotional tensions that are carried by the body. If you give the relaxation exercises a try, you can find out which parts of your body are chronically stiff and anxious. You might try massaging the affected regions, but be careful not to overstretch any of the muscles.

You may find that joining both hands behind your head, bringing the shoulders back, and pressing your head into your hands helps relieve stress in the neck. Try to exert as much force as you can with both hands. If you find that you have chronic tension in your body, it may be time to reevaluate your lifestyle. Are you more of a sedentary person? Do you often go to bed without having even attempted to exercise? Keep in mind that releasing any areas of physical tension can help you sit more easily once you start meditating on the topic.

It is important to breathe from the diaphragm.

A lot of individuals don't pay any attention to how they breathe. One of the most essential skills to acquire before beginning meditation is the ability to remain still. Place one hand on the top part of your chest and breathe normally. Observe the rise and fall of your chest as you breathe in and out. When you meditate, you will become aware that you are breathing deliberately, paying special attention to the rhythmic cycle of your breath and even noticing how your lungs, belly, and diaphragm rise and fall in response to each inhale and exhale.

When you breathe in, take a long, deep breath in through your nose, and hold it for as long as you can until it reaches your belly and then goes through your diaphragm. When you exhale, the pattern should be turned upside down. Make sure to keep an eye out for the little pause that occurs between each inhale and exhale, and focus on feeling each breath move through your abdomen.

The significance of practicing breath counting

This is a well-known method for bringing one's mental and physical self into harmony with one another. When counting your breaths, it is important to retain a mental count of the number of breaths you take without being sidetracked or losing track of the count. This is a fantastic exercise that may also be used in meditation. Start by going through the numbers one through ten in your head. When you feel like you've got the hang of it, try counting as you take a breath in. That would make up one of them. When you let out your breath, it will count as two. Repeat this counting method until it becomes second nature to you.

It is stated that counting your breaths is a wonderful way to prepare your mind for meditation since it teaches your mind to be more attentive.

Meditation Techniques

There are thousands of various ways to meditate, and each one may help you achieve the stillness and inner peace that you've been searching for. The whole of these various approaches may be grouped together under a total of five distinct primary headings. These classifications are as follows:

Meditation on the Art of Concentration
Meditation on Being Present or Mindful
Meditation on Creativity
Meditation on Self-Reflection
Meditation that Is Focused on the Heart

The majority of individuals, and especially novices, turn to concentration meditation as a means to assist them relax and reduce tension. Let's take a look at each of the several approaches to meditation that are available.

Meditation Methods That Focus On Concentration

The practice of all other forms of meditation is made possible by first mastering the concentration meditation technique. When you have developed your capacity for mental concentration to such a degree that you are able to overcome any and all distractions and concentrate clearly on a single subject, you have achieved a state known as "flow." Our mind is tremendously strong, yet it is often disorganized due to the fact that it is always thinking about a myriad of various things. You will be able to make your mind more strong and set yourself free when you are able to completely submerge yourself in the mental state in which you are able to block out what you do not want and bring in more good ideas and feelings. Concentration meditation is one method that may be used to assist in the reduction of stress in one's life, as well as the accompanying feelings of concern and anxiety.

Meditation with full awareness

The next style of meditation that is most often done is called mindful meditation. When you meditate with awareness, you are able to focus more intently, resulting in a stronger connection to and comprehension of the wonderful things that exist in the world. Your ability to enjoy the world and all that it has to offer is directly correlated to your level of success in practicing mindful meditation.

Meditation on Creativity

People who desire to reduce the amount of stress in their lives might get benefits from practicing creative meditation as well. When you practice creative meditation, you open yourself up to the possibility of fully feeling the marvels of love, admiration, gratitude, and compassion for other people. After you have completed this process of meditation with success, you will have a greater knowledge of those incredible feelings that we all experience on the inside. These characteristics will all of a sudden spring to life inside us, helping to develop us intellectually and physically while also allowing us to create stronger connections not just with the people we love but also with the world around us.

Meditation on Self-Reflection

Meditation on reflection enables us to train our ideas and bring them under control. Reflective meditation gives you the ability to refocus your attention on the issue at hand whenever you notice that your thoughts have wandered off subject. Those who are going through a stressful time may benefit by meditating and reflecting on their experiences. When you practice reflective meditation, you may have a deeper understanding of life and what it's all about. Reflective meditation can help you see things more clearly. You now have a heightened awareness of both your surroundings and your own life, as well as an increased social consciousness. You may also use reflective meditation to assist you in locating internal difficulties and working through them.

Meditation that Is Focused on the Heart

The fifth primary kind of meditation is known as meditation with the focus on the heart. This kind of meditation involves the use of practices that help you awaken your innate capacity for love and compassion. You will become kinder, nicer, and more loving after you have successfully mastered this form of meditation and can call it your own. You will be more empathetic toward other people's predicaments and more forgiving of those who have wronged you. You will have the ability to think on your life in a creative manner and to listen intently to the words that other people have to say as they are said.

There are advantages to be gained by practicing any kind of meditation. However, if you want to get rid of stress, it is probably reasonable to state that concentration meditation gives the greatest set of advantages of all the different types of meditation. Choosing the style of meditation that works best for your requirements is totally up to you. Through the practice of meditation, one is able to transcend their regular condition and satisfy their most inner goals and wants. You may take control of your thoughts and the way you see the world around you via the practice of meditation. If you practice meditation on a consistent basis, it will unquestionably assist you in figuring out what the real purpose of life is. You won't have to worry about experiencing stress anymore, at least not to the same degree as you formerly did.

Your life can be transformed by meditation, but only if you are prepared to open yourself up to such transformations. Try some meditation if you've ever been curious about what it might be like to have an experience of being outside of your body. It is a great sense of mental happiness, and before you realize it, you will be in a continual state of serenity rather than tension. You may achieve this state of mental bliss by practicing mindfulness.

What Exactly Does It Mean When Someone Says They Are Mindful, And In What Ways May It Benefit You?

Meditation is practicing being fully present in the here and now. Simply directing your attention, on a moment-to-moment basis, to the experience of the here and now is the essence of this practice. When you are attentive, you are consciously taking in all that you feel, see, and smell in the present moment. When you practice mindfulness, you are actively and deliberately bringing your attention to the here and now. Being aware is paying deliberate attention in the present moment to the sensations, thoughts, and emotions that arise as a result of whatever activity you find yourself engaged in.

To provide a concrete illustration of this idea, let's use something as inconsequential as eating as our example. When you eat with a mindful approach, you are aware of more than just the food that you are consuming. When you are present in the moment and conscious of what you are doing, including eating, you pay attention to the experience itself. You are paying close attention to the feelings that you are experiencing right now. If you become aware that your thoughts have wandered off while you are eating, you should consciously direct your focus back to the food that you are chewing as well as the feelings that you are experiencing while you are eating.

But why should one engage in mindfulness practice? What are some of the advantages that might come from practicing awareness via meditation?

The practice of mindfulness has been shown to promote overall well-being. People who are more aware and present in their lives are happier and more fulfilled as a result of the fact that they take the time to notice the smallest of details. When you are attentive, you are able to relish and take pleasure in each moment; as a consequence, you develop a greater sense of contentment, gratitude, and overall happiness. Your ability to deal with difficult and upsetting experiences that life may throw at you is bolstered when you practice mindfulness.

Your mental health may benefit from practicing mindfulness because when you are attentive, you have a greater degree of mental control. You may have more control over your mind and thoughts by developing the skill of mindfulness meditation and practicing it regularly. When you train your mind to be attentive, it becomes much simpler to recognize unhelpful thoughts and to replace them with more constructive ones. When you are attentive, you have less preoccupation and are less impacted by the errors you've made in the past. Numerous studies have shown that practicing mindfulness may be beneficial in reducing symptoms of drug misuse, anxiety disorders, and eating disorders.

Mindfulness is beneficial to your physical health since it reduces stress and teaches you to relax more effectively. Your general health will improve as a direct consequence of this. Your blood pressure will decrease, the quality and duration of your sleep will improve, and it will also assist soothe any difficulties you have with your digestive system.

It is well recognized that practicing mindfulness may strengthen relationships since it lowers the amount of emotional volatility experienced by the practitioner. When you are attentive, you tend to have less of a critical attitude toward other people and more tolerance for the errors that others make. Additionally, it develops compassionate attitudes.

The practice of mindfulness may help you feel more connected to both yourself and the world around you. If you practice mindfulness meditation, you will become more in tune with both your emotions and your thoughts, which will allow you to learn more about who you are as a person as a direct consequence of this practice. You have a closer relationship with the person you are.

Meditation focusing on awareness of the present moment is a common component in behavioral treatments and psychotherapies. It is a method that has been shown via research to make one's life better. When you practice mindfulness, you do not just float or glide through life; rather, you actively participate in it. You are living each moment, and as you do so, you come to the realization and observation that life is, in fact, extremely lovely.

Incorrect Functioning of Our Fifth Chakra

When we realize that we have a desire to express ourselves, but instead of doing so in a way that would win the acceptance and approval of others, we try to persuade and force our beliefs on others on the grounds that "they are the ones that are right." This is one of the instances at which there is an imbalance. We start to speak in a manner that is diametrically opposed to what the majority of people say. If they say white, then I will say black, and that will be the truth for everyone! There is no discrimination nor understanding; only imposition. It is important to emphasize that the goal of our fifth Chakra is not to force our will on others but rather to express ourselves.

One further thing to consider is our natural reluctance to express oneself. Staying in the house is the best option, even though we have a million things running through our heads and the want to get some fresh air. Put an end to your worry that others do not have the same viewpoint as you. Because of this, we will be relegated to the role of spectators at all of the meetings in which we participate, and our presence will be noted only as a "ghost." There is just the jail available to the fifth Chakra if it desires release. When was the last time you had a fantastic idea that you didn't have the courage to implement, only to find out that "someone won"? That would be the end effect of someone being afraid to express themselves.

A further indicator of an imbalance in this Chakra is the inability to get control over stage fright. When we make an effort to reduce this energy rather than capitalize on it, which throws us off-kilter and causes us to lose equilibrium, the energy cannot be switched off or concealed since it is just there. What we are able to do is exert control over it and utilize it to our advantage.

Keeping the Check and Balance
When our fifth Chakra is in a state of equilibrium, we are able to fully distinguish all aspects of the world around us and experience life with an abundance of pleasure and a sense of renewed vigor. If you are an artist, you are able to create quality and originality;

if you are in love, you will fill your relationship with details that will avoid routine and custom; and if you are a trader, you will have the vision to take your company to the summit if you are creative. Creativity is reflected in each of your actions, and they flow continuously, they do not stop.

This occurs when you feel confident in your own identity, when you are conscious of yourself and of the power that you possess, and when there are no anxieties or insecurities present. Your mental state shifts to one in which it is liberated, open, untethered, and self-sufficient; it is aware of who it is, and it no longer perceives the many perspectives that are there as a danger.
You will start looking for quality time, parties and everyday amusements will no longer be attractive, and you will look for solitude and introspection instead. At this point, your social life may be different; it is certain that you are bored with "superficial" issues, and you will start rejecting situations in which this

occurs. You won't get together to watch the football game anymore; instead, you'll work toward integrating with the individuals who question "the match of life."

What the Soul of the Fifth Chakra Is Trying to Communicate

The higher Chakras are communal in character, and they provide a connection between ourselves and the more evolved dimension of our species. Your unique combination of individual and communal experiences positions you as a wellspring of original ideas. You have the ability to jolt many individuals out of their slumber, and rather than following predetermined routes, you should pursue your own individuality and forge your own path.

People will look to you as a model for their own lives to emulate if you take the initiative to seek out an open stance on the truth. They will eventually discover their own identities as a direct result of his beginning to doubt who he is.

Activities That Will Help You Awaken the Fifth Chakra

The first workout

Consider the practice of "the rod of talk," which is common in many different kinds of organizations, if you suffer from public speaking anxiety or are reluctant to share your thoughts. When you have something to say, you may command your wand to speak, and everyone will listen carefully to what it has to say. You may do this by visualizing a wand, having something to say at all times, and not being scared to act upon what you've visualized.

Workout number 2

Imagine that you are working on a project and you run into a wall of blocked energy. This is what it feels like when your creativity is "blocked." This may occasionally occur when there is still a little imbalance in one or more of our Chakras. Allow your creativity and energy to flow freely by taking a few deep breaths into the throat chakra.

The Aina, or Sixth Chakra

Indigo blue is the color.

Fluorite, indigo tourmaline, and other crystals

Place: in the frown

When our sixth chakra begins to open, we are overcome by an intense want to experience the enchantment of a reality that transcends our own. A reality that is neither typical or commonplace, but rather one that is vast and unbounded. The vehicle for this transcendence is imagination; here, mental pictures are coupled with an inner power that insists on knowing all; this combination is an inspiration and brings both good luck and fortune.

A properly directed imagination may provide an escape from the mundane realities of everyday life, allowing one to establish a connection with the holy and with feelings that extend beyond the sensory realm. We can use our imagination as a form of expansion and transcendence. Another way is to use television as a means of evasion, and although it is not so harmful, it limits our field of action. The time and energy that we dedicate to entertainment is the same time that we could use to start putting together our projects. When we talk about leaks, we are also talking about risks.

vices such as drugs and alcohol are examples of harmful vices.
When we awaken in our sixth Chakra, we also awaken our intuition, which serves as a guide to help us follow our path. By working with our imagination, we are able to distinguish what we enjoy, as well as what gives us energy and what drains us of it. When we follow the paths that connect us with our nature and our identity, we can be certain that we are following our own light. We are going about things incorrectly when we are adamant about living a life that we do not want to live, one that overpowers and displeases us.

while we want to awaken our intuition, we need to do it with spiritual will, also known as the will of faith. We can no longer allow ourselves to experience dread while making decisions; instead, we need to reserve our anxieties for indications of genuine danger rather than using them as a way of life. Faith is what matters most in this situation, both faith in what it is that we desire and confidence that we are on the right route to get there.

In order to identify what our intuition dictates, all you need to do is ask yourself whether what you are doing or what you are going to do links you to your energy flow, if there is progress or degradation, and if it is healthy or unhealthy. whether the answer to any of these questions is "yes," then you are on the right track to recognizing what our intuition dictates.

There is no longer any judging or criticizing, things cease being good or terrible, and we just view them as a variety of ways of being and thinking. Our sixth Chakra assists us in the creation of a collective consciousness;

we begin to function as spectators or observers of what occurs to us and of ideology in general; there are no longer any judgements or critiques.

Getting Back In Touch With Your Developing Intuition

It is essential that you establish a connection with your intuition before you begin developing your psychic talents, since this will serve as your guide throughout the process. As you become more attuned to what your senses are conveying to you and have the ability to put more faith in them, this connection between the two of you will eventually become stronger and more profound. When you are aware of the indications, you will be able to start seeing the messages that are being sent to you by your body via your intuition. You will need to pay very close attention because we can hear a voice in our minds that we label as intuition, but it might really be your ego attempting to fool you into thinking that it is alright to do what you ultimately intended to do in the first place. You will need to pay very close attention because we can hear a voice in our minds that we label as intuition.

Creating a visualization is a great approach to practice reconnecting with or enhancing your intuitive abilities. Imagine you are in a coffee shop catching up with an old buddy from your childhood who you haven't seen since you were a kid. You are both enjoying a drink. You and your childhood friend(s) rehash all of the tales that you used to talk about when you were younger and use this time to catch up on your own life experiences. Because of these chats, you are able to recall the dynamic of the personal connection that you had with them all of this time ago; nonetheless, it seems as if you had not spent so much time away from each other.

Despite this, you have a sense of distance between you and the other person due to the diverse experiences that you and the other person have had, and you see each other as strangers in this respect. To be able to alleviate this sense of isolation, you will need to reacquaint yourself with your buddy on the basis of who they are right now rather than on the basis of who they were in your recollection.

In the same manner that you would talk to an old friend from your childhood, you need to approach your intuition in the same way. From this vantage point, you are able to realize that your intuition has always been a component of who you are, despite the fact that you may have pursued numerous paths and lost touch with it over the years. On the other hand, it is never impossible to restart this connection with your intuition and get it back on track. You will discover that you will be able to grow this connection in a very personal manner if you are able to spend the time each day to work on this relationship just as you would with any other person and you will find that you will be able to do so with any other individual as well.

The Physiological Repercussions of Prolonged Stress

the effects on the neurological system. You are going to discover that all of the tension that has been subtly working its way into your system is really doing you a great deal more damage than you ever imagined it could. If the chronic stress that you are putting yourself through is not brought under control in a timely manner, you run the risk of being exposed to high levels of anxiety, which is a very real possibility. In addition, anxiety is a forerunner to the distressing illness of depression, and when you discover that you are tormented by all of this, you may find that it is difficult to get out of bed and go to work at all, which will, in turn, undermine all of the hard work that you put into increasing your productivity at the workplace.

Heart problems. You put yourself at a higher risk of developing cardiovascular disease if you allow stress to build up to the point where it becomes unmanageable. This is mostly attributable to the high-fat, high-salt foods that provide individuals with a momentary sense of solace and, at first glance, seem to mitigate the unfavorable consequences of stress and anxiety. If you are not cautious, then over time you might significantly raise the likelihood of having a stroke, which is something you never imagined your hectic work life could be capable of leading to.

Elevated levels of blood pressure. This condition is also referred to as hypertension. Your chance of having a stroke, heart failure, renal failure, and cardiovascular disease is significantly enhanced when your blood pressure skyrockets due of the elevated amounts of stress in your life. This puts you in a very precarious situation. In any case, stress will result in a rise in blood pressure over the course of a short length of time, but it becomes a significant issue when it lasts for an extended period of time; chronic stress may lead to hypertension, which you need to prevent at all costs by taking action right now to reduce it!

vulnerability to many diseases and conditions. You put yourself at risk for a wide variety of ailments simply due to the fact that the strain that your mind and body are under causes your immune system to become compromised. Aside from that, being stressed out also makes the process of recovering from any sickness that you could be suffering from go more slowly.

Meditation while standing
Sitting meditation is far more common than standing meditation. In most cases, it is performed during a period of walking meditation. Imagine you have to stand for a significant amount of time. It seems like something that would have been really challenging for me to do.

Stop whatever you're doing and take some time to collect your thoughts if you find that you're losing your consciousness while you're out walking. This would buy you some time to gather your thoughts. After that, you may continue with your stroll.

If you find that you are becoming exhausted from all of the walking but are not quite ready to conclude your meditation, you may always stop and stand for a minute.

If you are walking and suddenly have an intriguing thought come to your head, stop what you are doing and stand there so that you may notice it more thoroughly.

I really hope that you have realized by this point that the objective of meditation is to make things easier for you. Therefore, you should engage in whatever seems the most natural and comfortable to you.

Meditation practiced while supine

Lying down to meditate is one of the most effective positions for developing one's capacity for focused attention. Some individuals believe that this position is really more beneficial to focus than sitting on a chair all day.

On the other hand, this environment makes it easier to fall asleep. When you meditate while laying down, maintaining consciousness should be your primary focus so that you do not fall asleep.

For walking meditation, the processes of taking a mental inventory, concentrating on the flow of breath, and ending the practice are identical to those for sitting meditation.

The Third Chapter

The Nine Aspects or States of Consciousness

In a previous section of this book, it was said that Buddhism is about gaining a knowledge of life. Because one cannot have an experience without consciousness, a proper comprehension of existence must begin with an awareness of what consciousness is and how it works. When we don't have a good grasp of awareness, it's impossible for us to comprehend what it is to be alive. Instead, we put ourselves in a position to experience sorrow when we buy into the illusions that our own brains have concocted. When we give in to the mind's warping of the world around us, we open ourselves up to the possibility of experiencing suffering. Buddhism has established models that may assist us in gaining a deeper comprehension of awareness.

The Nichiren school of Buddhism is known for its use of a paradigm called the Nine Consciousnesses. This model not only helps us get a better grasp of the nature of consciousness, but it also helps us gain a deeper understanding of our real nature, our Buddha nature, which is enlightenment. Both of these benefits are very beneficial to us. When Shakyamuni Buddha was meditating under the Bodhi tree more than 2,500 years ago, he suddenly became aware of the real essence of things. This is the same true nature that I speak about.

One way to think about the Nine Consciousnesses is as different levels of awareness. We will begin with the most superficial layer and work our way down to the most profound layer, which is our natural state of enlightenment.

Levels of Consciousness 1–5

The five senses—sight, smell, hearing, touch, and taste—comprise the first five layers of the onion. The role served by these five levels of awareness is that of receiving information from our surrounding environment. These five sensory modalities are the channels through which we perceive life. The sixth layer, often known as the sixth awareness, is responsible for processing the raw material provided by the information that we get from different sensory modalities.

The Sixth Level of Consciousness

The sixth layer of consciousness is responsible for synthesizing the information that was obtained from the preceding five levels and incorporating it into a comprehensive representation or idea. My eyes take in all the visual information that my dog presents to me whenever he approaches me. My sense of hearing enables me to take in the sound of him barking, while my sense of smell enables me to take in information on whether or not he needs a wash. When I pet him, it stimulates my sense of touch, which enables me to gather information. My brain compiles each of these distinct pieces of information into a cohesive whole, which I refer to simply as a "dog." When we are engaged in our day-to-day activities, we spend the majority of our time operating inside the first six levels of awareness.

The Seventh Level of Consciousness

The seventh level of consciousness may be found layered underneath the sixth level of awareness. The first six levels of consciousness have an outward emphasis, which means that they are oriented toward the external world. The seventh layer of consciousness, on the other hand, is where we experience our feeling of identity, as well as our attachments to a distinct sense of self and our judgements. Both my sense of who I am as a person and my feeling that I am an independent entity from my dog, or anybody else, originate from the seventh awareness. This is also true for any other individual. This is also the source of my beliefs, values, and judgements.

The Octave of Consciousness

The eighth consciousness, also known as alaya-vijnana, is the next lower level of consciousness after the seventh. The eighth awareness functions as a repository for the karmic energy that we have. The eighth awareness stores the recollection of each and every event that we have ever experienced throughout our whole existence. As a result of this, it has an effect on all of the layers that are above it.

Memory, desire, and action all play a part in the cycle that gives rise to karmic energy. My dog always brings up fond recollections of times spent with him. These recollections spark a longing inside me, a want to rekindle my relationship with him. A result of this desire is that I pet him. The completion of the circle is brought about by the formation of fresh recollections as a result of my touching him. In a similar manner, the quality of the imprints that my previous experiences have made in the eighth awareness is what determines the nature of the life that I experience.

The karmic energies of the eighth consciousness impact the seventh consciousness in such a way that it affects any judgements that I may have towards my dog, which in turn influences the first five levels of awareness. If my evaluations of my dog, which are heavily impacted by my memories of him, are positive, then I will perceive him differently than I would if my recollections of him were negative.

In contrast to the earlier levels of consciousness, which vanish when a person dies, the eighth layer of awareness is everlasting and will continue to exist even after we do. It will do so by occupying various forms, which is what is often known as reincarnation. It is a person's karma, not the person themselves, that determines whether or not they will have another life. This karma is something that is passed down from person to person, particularly through families, communities, and racial and ethnic groups. To modify one's karma via growing clarity about the workings of the mind and the actual nature of the self is one of the key reasons to practice Buddhist meditation. This clarity may be gained through meditation. In the same way as the dawning of a new day obscures the night sky with stars, the cultivation of awareness via prolonged meditation purges all of the karma that stands between us and the realization of genuine calm.

The Ninth Level of Consciousness

Amala consciousness, also known as the ninth consciousness, is the next lower level of awareness after the eighth consciousness. The ninth awareness is free of any and all karmic influences; it is a state of unadulterated consciousness. The ninth awareness has an endless potential to materialize into form, and it has been around from the beginning of time. In a deeper sense, it is our essential character. At this level, all of us come together to form a single, indivisible creature. When we build our lives on the ninth consciousness and carry out our lives via the first five levels, we feel genuine freedom and pleasure. This is the ultimate objective of Buddhist meditation, which is to directly recognize the ninth consciousness.

How to Meditate to Deepen Your Spirituality and Simplify Your Life is the Topic of Chapter 6 of this Book.

When you meditate often, you clear the mental clutter that's been building up inside of you, and as a result, your life becomes easier and less confusing. Increasing your sense of fulfillment may also be accomplished in the following ways:

1. Get rid of all the chaos — Although meditation helps you to get rid of the chaos in your head, if you want to live a simpler life, you also need to get rid of the chaos around you. Disorganization is a fundamental contributor to feelings of tension and anxiety. Clearing the clutter

from your life will also clear the clutter from your thinking.

2. Simplify your conception of what it means to be successful. If you will only consider yourself successful if you have a fortune of one billion dollars, you will never be content. Make your idea of success more grounded in reality and less focused on acquiring material things.

3. Make the most of what you have - Meditation may help you control your wants and desires, which makes it easier to make the most of what you have. If you do not live within your means, you will accumulate debt, and this may be a source of a great deal of worry for you throughout your life. Do not put yourself in financial ruin in an effort to impress other people.

4. Acquire a deeper understanding of the notion of "enough" Meditation may help you become more at peace with who you are and where you are in life. You may

also improve this ability by becoming more familiar with the meaning of the phrase "enough" Do not put undue pressure on yourself to acquire items that you do not genuinely need.

5. Learn to Forgive - Meditating can help you become more receptive to the idea of forgiving others. It is necessary for you to release all of the resentment that you have inside your heart in order to make your life more fulfilling and less complex. Always keep in mind that the act of forgiving others will bring happiness and a sense of fulfillment to your life.

6. retain an open mind — If you want to live a life that is more fascinating and enjoyable, you need to retain an open mind. Think on the perspectives and judgments of other people, since it's possible that they're correct.
7. Acquire the skill of delegation and avoid becoming a micromanager. Have faith that other people will take care of

things for you. It will make things a great deal less difficult for you.

8. Smiling - There is no physical or mental strain that can compete with the power of a smile. Your life will become easier and more enjoyable once you realize you don't need to sweat the little stuff and simply smile.

Increased spirituality is only one of the several advantages that comes with regular meditation practice. When you make meditation a regular part of your life and practice mindfulness and focus on a consistent basis, you get closer to the Divine and the Creator.

You may develop a closer relationship with the one who created you by using the following meditation technique:

1. Ensure that you are seated in a posture that is comfortable and shut your eyes.

2. Taking a few slow, deep breaths, inhaling with your nose and exhaling through your mouth, can help you relax and center yourself.

3. Invoke the presence of the Creator by offering a brief prayer of thanksgiving.

4. While you are breathing in and out, repeat the word "God" to yourself. In the event that your thoughts start to wander, return your attention back to the word "God." Continue doing this for ten to fifteen minutes.

5. At the end of your meditation session, offer a brief prayer expressing thankfulness to the universe.

6. Make this part of your regular routine.

It is important to keep in mind that one of the most common types of meditation is prayer. When you pray to the Divine and the Creator, avoid using a pattern, and don't make any requests for specific items. Make sure that your prayer has a conversational tenor to it. You will feel more connected to the Divine Power as you engage in this activity.

Meditation is one of the many practices that might bring a person closer to the Divine. Another kind of meditation is called mindfulness. When you practice mindfulness and you live in the present now, you have the opportunity to notice things that you have taken for granted in the past, such as the air that you breathe, the lovely flowers that are growing in your yard, and the other things and people that you are blessed with. When you cultivate mindfulness and focus on being present in the moment, you more often find yourself awestruck by the incredible work of the creator, and as a consequence, you feel a stronger connection to the Divine.

How Are You Supposed To Read This Book?

Because each chapter will be devoted to a different guided meditation, you are not need to read the book in any particular sequence in order to get the most out of it. I will explain in detail at what points in the meditation you should take a break and for how long you should do so. If you want to read this book, the only need is that you should be able to relax in a quiet setting free from interruptions.

CHAPTER 1: A Brief and Powerful Guided Meditation (five minutes that will change your life)
The purpose of this guided meditation is to induce a state of concentration in a short amount of time. You'll get the finest results if you do it every day.

Take a full breath and count to thirty. Straighten out your back to allow your breath to come in a more natural way.

Don't stress out about maintaining ideal posture. Simply realign your spine so that you can breathe more easily for twenty seconds. Put your hands in a position that allows you to relax as you put your feet up on the floor. You have twenty seconds to close your eyes and concentrate on being aware of your breathing. Take a few deep breaths, then let yourself relax. Pay close attention to the air coming in and leaving for a period of twenty seconds. Take a few deep breaths and try to relax.

Put out of your mind any and all ideas that are attempting to divert your attention, and concentrate solely. Try to find somewhere quiet and relaxing to spend your time. Make yourself at home and take it easy. Take a deep breath in and hold it for thirty seconds. Relax and focus on the sensation of the air entering your body with each breath you take. Maintain your focus on the way you are breathing. Let rid of the things that aren't required, the things that are making your life more difficult, and the things that you've been dragging about for a very long time (20 seconds). Take a deep breath in and then out. Refresh yourself, let rid of everything that prevents your life from moving forward, and release all of the emotions that keep you from growing as a person. You've been dragging around some unneeded feelings for a long time; it's time to let them go. You may make your trip easier on yourself by letting go of stuff that you should have left behind earlier. Take a long, deep breath in, and then let out as much air as you can after a count of thirty.

Be present at this moment, breathe (20 seconds) keep your attention on the here and now. Inhale, then exhale for a count of thirty. 20 seconds should be spent on releasing all of your physical and mental stress with each breath. Take a deep breath in and then out. Feel the tension leaving your body. Take another deep breath in (twenty-twenty seconds). Pay attention to the activities that are occurring on the inside of you. The resources that you now possess are sufficient to ensure that you will be OK. Don't live attached to the illusion that something is missing to be happy.

There is nothing outside of you that can fill the phony sensation of emptiness, and this is only a notion that restricts your overall growth. It is just an illusion created by your mind, which is filled with worry about the future and a need for safety. Appreciate the moments of your life and be grateful for them as they occur. Inhale slowly, exhale. (30 seconds). Be grateful for your life. Breathe and just focus on the movement of your breath. Inhale, exhale (20 seconds).

Take another deep breath in (twenty-twenty seconds).

The Peace and Quiet of the Shower as a Sanctuary

My home in New Orleans is a two-bedroom home, and I consider myself quite fortunate to have a wonderful spare room that is furnished with books, plants, Buddhas, and a cozy space dedicated to meditation. It is adorable and reassuring, and the dark crimson color that it is painted gives it a little bit of a mysterious air. On the other hand, I can state without a shred of irony that the shower is the place in the home where I experience the greatest serenity. Without a doubt.

Because a tree casts its shadow on the glass of the restroom, the room is never too light. I adorned the window panels with a flower-themed film, which throws various colours of pink, orange, and red onto the tiling. I removed all of the clutter from the shower, except for one bar of soap that was displayed on a soap dish in the shape of a purple elephant.

Because of the limited size of the room and the way the shower is discretely built into the next wall, the atmosphere exudes an air of warm invitation. The movement of water has a naturally calming effect, and if you shut your eyes, you may easily fool yourself into thinking that you are standing in front of a waterfall at the peak of a mountain or in the saline passageways of a cave near the ocean.

When I was younger, all of this began to happen. Because I used up all of the hot water, I may get into trouble. I swore to you that I could remain in there for a whole hour. I can still hear my parents yelling at me to hurry up and get ready to go. Even though I've become much more aware of the environment, my favorite way to unwind is still to lie down and let all of that steam and hot water fall over me like a million little raindrops.

Bringing your attention to the present moment during mundane activities like brushing your teeth or washing your hair may be as easy as taking a mindful shower. The following are a few different approaches that may help you get the most out of it: *

The concept of letting the water "wash your day away" is a common method, and it may be a particularly helpful transitional aid if you go into the water right after you come home from work. You are probably aware that there are days when you may leave work and everything will still be there, but on most days, we bring a lot of junk home with us. Your mood may be quickly lifted by taking a shower after removing your work clothes and imagining that all of your problems – anything that was said to worry you, a deadline that you are worried about, and any sensations of discomfort – are washing down the drain. This can help you get over anything that was said to disturb you at work. Put an end to pondering such things. Observe how they whirl about and eventually disappear. Give them some space.

Of course, we are not really attempting to make any problems associated with real life vanish into thin air. But by helping yourself make the mental shift from work to home with this image, you are enabling yourself to let go of the load so that you may totally relax and concentrate on something else. It is a ritualistic reminder to let all of those anxieties drop away so that you may genuinely enjoy your time off, read your book in peace, and play with your children in peace.

The same is true for every day, regardless of whether or not you have to work. Even when we are having a good day, we still carry thoughts with us and keep ourselves preoccupied by constantly going over the events of the day in our brains. Although there is nothing intrinsically wrong with it, having too much of it might prevent us from living fully in the here and now. Put all of that behind you so you may concentrate on the things that are occurring in the here and now.
Alternately, if you are the kind of person who always takes a shower first thing in

the morning, you may see this ritual as a way to start fresh with your life. You should try to relax your muscles as well as your thoughts, and you should imagine that whatever worries you have about the day will just melt away.

Even when I'm in the shower, I'll sometimes remark out loud to myself, "You're home." There are times when all you need is a little nudge.

The next method is the tool for mindfulness that I consider to be my personal favorite. The purpose of this is to draw attention to each of the five senses. I always make it a point to do this whenever I go in the shower, even if it's only going to be a fast rinse. In addition, this is the one method that I always do, even if I'm having a bad day. It never fails to make me feel better. It is really peaceful, and I find that it is especially beneficial when I am feeling nervous since, by following the steps, it is temporarily hard for me to remain focused on my problems. This makes it particularly useful for me when I am feeling anxious. Even though it was just for a few while, I was able to experience a brightening of my mood as well as a lifting of my spirit when I took a break from the constant looping of my thoughts. It is up to you whether you choose to spend a short amount of time on each stage or sensation, or if you would rather take your time to absorb what you are seeing, smelling, feeling, tasting, and hearing.

And to do this, you should perform the following (in any order):

1. SEE. Choose something that will definitely catch your eye. It might be the light coming in through the holes in the shower curtain, or it could be a little chip in the tile. It might be the bright green color of the soap, however. If you want to take your bathing experience to the next level, try using one of those bath bombs. As it dissolves into the water, it will spin and swirl, creating a rainbow of colors. Take a closer look at something and do it with a greater level of interest than you would ordinarily.

2. THE ODOR. Choose an item that has a strong aroma. In a typical scenario, I will

cup my hands in front of my face, inhale deeply, and take in the invigorating aroma of new soap. Take note of if it has a fragrance reminiscent of fruit or perfume, as well as whether it evokes any recollections of other odors. You might also try cracking open the cap of your shampoo or even smelling the water to see if it has any odor.

3. FEEL. Choose something that touches you deeply. A simple example of this would be being aware of the sensation of hot water on your back or your hands, or of the feeling of tiles or porcelain under your feet. Touch the tile, the rounded curvature of the bar of soap, and the little elevation at the label's edge of the bottle of shampoo you are using.

4. THE TASTE 5. Choose something you can appreciate the flavor of. This one calls for a little of imagination on your part, but what I like to do is take a minute to concentrate on the flavor that is now there in my tongue. It may be coffee, it could be something sweet, or it could be hints of a variety of tastes all combined together. Putting your focus to

something that you previously hadn't noticed may help you become aware of a flavor that you were previously oblivious to.

5. HEAR. Choose something that will truly get your attention. My go-to technique for this is to cup my hand, press it against my ear, and then let the water to drip into the cup created by my hand. I shut my eyes and listen to the sound of water trickling down, just like raindrops hitting a canvas shelter.

You should give this workout a go every time you step into the shower. I'll repeat it one more: you don't need to spend an excessive amount of time doing this. Just a few seconds to re-center yourself and intentionally refocus your attention to the time at hand by focusing on each of your senses in turn.

The Harmful Effects of Both Giving and Receiving

I have gone into a lot of detail above about how it is necessary for us to accept whatever it is that our parents have provided for us in its current form. However, there are certain occurrences or happenings that are the responsibility of the parents and are the result of their own personal circumstances. These include financial duties and debts, any calamitous events befalling the parent such as sickness, and any personal profits or losses acquired as a result of one's own efforts, whether positive or negative. There are certain families in which the son feels responsible to pay off the debts incurred by the parent. The kid does not need to feel the necessity or responsibility to do so in these situations; rather, the youngster should respond, "This is your heavy fate Dad, and not mine." You are responsible for paying off this loan." This will release the youngster from their confinement. However, if the kid continues to pay off the debt that the father owes, then it is an unhealthy pattern of giving and receiving between the two of them. In circumstances like these, the kid's father should make it clear to the youngster that the child is capable of handling his own problems. And in situations in which the biological father is no longer around, it is important for the kid to comprehend the concept that parents are significant and children are insignificant. Parents have the resources and abilities necessary to handle their own problems.

As parents, they have a responsibility to keep these things from their children and keep their children safe. And one does not have to endure these afflictions just because they are a youngster. When this sort of giving and receiving takes place, there is a disruption in the very core of life, and there is an interruption in the flow of love. Entangled is what happens to a young person who, out of blind love or unwavering allegiance to his parents, attempts to shoulder the heavy burden of his parents' destiny. The youngster begins to suffer as a result of his attempts to fulfill the suffering of his parents by taking their place inside the system and completing their ordeal. This is not conceivable since each individual occupies a distinct position within the system. There are times when the youngster is exhibiting the same difficulties and patterns in his life as his parents did at the same age. When this happens, the youngster becomes even more knotted up since there is no flow of LIFE FORCE ENERGY inside him. The system immediately initiates its own plan of action in order to correct the damaging giving and receiving that has occurred.

I would recommend that you conduct the meditation that is listed below as well as the movement of the soul in order to release any unhealthy habits of giving and receiving that may have developed with your parents.

Meditate on this:

1. Start by closing your eyes and taking a few long, deep breaths to clear your head. Take a deep breath and exhale all of the distracting ideas, sensations, and emotions. Take a deep breath and inhale love, harmony, and tranquility.

2. Give yourself permission to become grounded, and allow yourself to sense the flow of love working in harmony inside you.

3. Bring your parents into your mind's eye and gaze at them with love and tenderness. Behold them with the profound and unbridled love that lies dormant inside you for them.

4. In your head, whisper to your parents, "Mummy, Daddy," filled with affection. I offer you my appreciation, love, respect, and honor as I accept this life that you have given me. The way it is is OK with me. 5. Have the sensation that you are getting more love, more care, and more affection from them. I know that you will always give me more, and I also know that I will always receive more from you. Get a sense of the joy that comes from them showering you with more of their good. Allow this energy to circulate freely throughout you. Feel the kindness that you have gotten from them growing inside of you with each breath you take.

6. Once again, whisper these words to your mother and father deep inside your heart: "Mummy and Daddy, if I have taken your heavy fate knowingly or unknowingly, I give it back to you as it is

yours and it is rightfully yours." I have faith that you will find a solution."

7. And now, simply let go of everything that doesn't belong to you that you've stolen from your parents and breathe it out. Put an end to any form of exchange that has resulted in hurtful giving or receiving that has taken place between you and your parents. Exhale absolutely all that's in your lungs.

8. Once you feel as though you have completely let go of it after releasing it, just take one more deep breath and relax. Look once again into the eyes of your parents, but this time do it with an attitude of appreciation for all the life lessons and opportunities they have bestowed upon you. Tell them, "I treasure it and respect it." I am going to make something positive out of my existence, and I am going to create my own experiences.

9. It is now time to gaze beyond them at your ancestors who are standing behind them, your great grandparents who are standing behind them, and so on back

through the whole ancestral bloodline. They should all be bowed to for the privilege of receiving the gift of life, for life itself is emanating from all of them. Make a respectful and honorable bow to them.

10. And very far behind all of them is standing the LIFE FORCE ENERGY, which is providing life to all of them and traveling up to you. 11. Pay respect to this energy and tell it, "Thank you, for giving me this life."

11. As you gaze at this energy, which has been passed down through every generation until ultimately arriving at you, keep in mind that everyone is contributing to the service of this energy. And now it is your turn to be of assistance to life.

12. Express thanks and love to the ENERGY OF THE LIFE FORCE as well as to your ancestral heritage by genuflecting before them. Sense how this love penetrates every part of your body and fills you up completely. It is surrounding you in a manner that is both entire and comprehensive.

13. When you feel as if you have absorbed enough of this energy for yourself, say "Thank you."
14. After that, let this energy to fully meld with your being on all levels. After you get the sensation of being integrated, carefully and gently open your eyes.

Mantra Meditation

Another form of closed-ended meditation, this one has you concentrating on a mantra rather than, say, your breath as the one before it did. The purpose of this exercise is to train your mind to think in the desired manner and to attract beneficial events to you as a result of your efforts.

Choose any aspect of your life that you feel may need some work and write a constructive recommendation about it. If you want more cash, say "I am wealthy and abundant." If you want to be happy, you may say, "I draw happiness towards me easily." If you are stressed out, say "I am calm." If you want more wealth, say "I am wealthy and abundant."

Choose any uplifting mantra you choose—it may be as simple as a single word like "hope," "peace," or "kindness," for example—and say it over and over again during the whole session. After beginning with a one-minute session of mindful breathing meditation, transition into chanting your chosen mantra for anywhere between five and ten minutes. It is possible that after a few days of doing this, you will experience feelings that are more cheerful, serene, and tranquil than you did before.

Meditation with No End in Sight

You are not obliged to focus your thoughts on anything in particular while engaging in this simple technique.

Get comfortable in the contemplative posture you've chosen, and then relax your body and mind by thinking about anything that makes you feel better. When you are feeling better, give yourself permission to let your mind wander freely and concentrate on one subject at a time.

Allow your mind to travel in whatever way they want, from thinking about the ceiling fan to thinking about the vase that is sitting on the table to thinking about how your daughter smiled at you to thinking about why you don't feel happy in life; then notice each idea very carefully.

This technique will help you to relax and clear your thoughts so that you can focus better. When you take some time to relax, things that have been bothering you will often come to your attention. This enables you to better recognize your issues and find solutions to them. Just keep in mind that you should give each concept the appropriate amount of time before moving on to the next one.

After each session, you should make it a habit to jot down your reflections as well as an assessment of how well you performed throughout the exercise. This will allow you to go through your ideas and investigate them more thoroughly. Keep in mind that practicing on a consistent basis is necessary in order to get mastery over oneself.

Meditation With Clare Is An Easy-To-Follow Guided Practice Perfect For Novices And Busy People.

For persons who are new to meditation or who are otherwise time-pressed, guided meditation makes the practice simple and efficient.

An instructor may guide one person or a group of people in a number of different methods, including speaking in person or on a tape, and occasionally playing in the background gentle, calming music, sounds of nature, or both. Guidance can be offered for one or more persons.

You may find several videos online that will lead you through a calming meditation experience. Discover one that works well for you whether you're in your indoor or outdoor location. When I'm at the beach or walking through the woods near my house, I keep my mobile phone on me. I have a tape that I recorded that I like to play at the beginning of my seminars on vision boards.

Choose the narrator that you like listening to the most, someone who can make you feel both unique and at ease. The reason I bring this up is because there are a lot of people that engage in this practice out there. There are instances when I feel that the music is played at too high of a volume, or that their voice is not as soothing as I would want it to be. You shouldn't have to be concentrating on the speaker or the music in order to follow along.

To assist you in following along with the audio recording of my guided meditation that can be found on YouTube, I have provided the script for the meditation below. Be aware that there are a huge number of other recordings, either audio or video, that may be found on the internet.

You might try beginning with as little as five minutes or fewer every day. It is beneficial to your ability to concentrate. It provides you with a sensation of serenity while simultaneously minimizing or doing away with any sense of tension.

If you'd like, you may start a timer. It's possible that you'll give in to the sensation of happiness and lose track of the passage of time as a result.

Because the advantages of meditating much exceed the time spent doing so, you will inevitably find that you want to devote more time to the practice over time. You will begin to look forward to meditating anytime you have some spare time, and you will begin to consider it to be your new hobby.

This one clocks in at little under four minutes, approximately.

You can view it here: https://youtu.be/K8QrT3JP0aI

Have fun!

This is the script for the guided meditation that can be found in the YouTube video that was just mentioned, which is called Clare Hurst's Guided Meditation for Beginners and Busy People.

•

Find a relaxing and secure place to hang out in. Enjoy the sensation of the noises that are all around you.

• Find a comfortable position. You should try to assume the lotus position, or at the very least, sit with your legs crossed on a cushion. If you feel the urge to, you may recline or sit in a chair that is comfy.

•

Make a series of gentle nodding motions with your head, first forward and back, then side to side.

•

You may find it easier to concentrate if you close your eyes or gaze down.

-

Now, bring your attention to the way you are breathing.

- Inhale through your nose in a deliberate and deliberate manner. Feel the expansion in your gut.

- Exhale gently through your lips, letting go of any tension that may be building up in your body.

-

Feel the muscles in your face and forehead relax, as well as the loosening of your jaw and the unclinching of your teeth.

- Take a few long, slow breaths in through your nose. Feel the expansion in your gut.

- Exhale completely through your lips while you relax your shoulders and the rest of your body, but avoid slouching.

- Inhale gently while focusing on keeping your nostrils open. Become aware of the air entering your lungs.

- Exhale gradually while focusing on keeping your mouth open. When you take a deep breath, you should feel the tension leaving your neck and shoulders.

- Your mind will be filled with a constant stream of thoughts. Just accept them and bring your attention back to your breathing.

- Become aware of the movement of your stomach, both in and out. Relax your shoulders and keep them motionless as you focus on breathing deeply from your diaphragm.

- With each breath, go down your body, expelling any tension that you may be feeling along the way.

- Allow your arms to relax all the way down to your fingers, and allow yourself to feel heavy as you exhale.

- Take a few deep breaths, focusing on filling your lungs with air as you slowly inhale through your nose.

- As you let your breath out, let a sensation of calm to spread from your chest to your stomach, hips, back, and legs, and then all the way down to your toes.

- As you let each breath out, your whole body should start to feel more relaxed.

-

Your reflections will return to you again.

- Do not focus on anything other than the way you are breathing.

- Inhale deeply through your nose and allow the air to completely fill your lungs.

- Exhale any emotions of stress that you may be experiencing via your mouth.

- As you focus on your breath, you should begin to experience feelings of relaxation and tranquility.

- You should have a healthy and happy feeling. As you continue to concentrate on your breathing, ideas come and go as they please.

-

Take some time to savor the calm and satisfaction that you're now experiencing.

- Take a deep breath in and then open your eyes.

- Let go of your breath, express appreciation as you stretch, and then gently get up.

The Practice Of Getting Ready To Meditate

.

To begin meditating, you will need a quiet space that is free from distractions where you may sit and focus without being disturbed. Therefore, you could decide to do it at home when no one else is present, or you might have a bedroom that is far from the craziness of everyday life where you know you won't be disturbed while you're working. Sounds coming from outside the room may be just as distracting as sounds coming from the street, so it's important to try to choose a spot where there isn't much that can pull your attention away from the practice of meditation. This will become less significant to you as you get more experience since your mind will be better educated to disregard all of the disruptions that life puts in the path of stillness. Pick a place to work in for the time being that will be quite quiet and won't provide many distractions.

Clothing used during meditative practices.
You are free to wear practically anything, but there are certain guidelines to follow. Do not put on anything that might possibly make you feel uncomfortable in any way. During your meditation, for instance, if you have a waistline that is too tight, this may bother you and cause your thoughts to wander away from the topic at hand, which is what you should be thinking about. Therefore, you should dress in loose, comfortable attire that won't constrict you in any manner. That includes one's undergarments as well. Change your underwear if you find that it is too constricting. Many of the ladies I know who meditate do so without wearing a bra because they believe it prevents them from breathing in the way that is most beneficial to them during the practice. Be sure that the clothes you choose to wear are

appropriate for the setting in which you will be meditating. You shouldn't let yourself become too warm or too chilly.

Placement inside the seat
This isn't nearly as significant as many people make it up to be in their minds. You really must assume a posture in which your back is perfectly straight. Meditation requires a certain posture to be maintained. You may, for instance, make yourself comfortable on a chair if your health is not in the best of shape. You may do yoga if you wish to and if you are already fit enough by purchasing a yoga cushion and using it. The most effective technique to get a good posture is to sit on a carpet or rug with your legs bent in front of you, then to cross your knees and arrange the cushion under your behind to make yourself as comfortable as possible. However, the cushion's primary function is to provide support for your posterior region. You are not required to purchase a yoga mat or a yoga cushion, but you have the option to do so. on any case – whether

you want to sit on the ground or on a chair - you need to ensure that you are comfortable.

Position of the hands
This is far more important than you may have first thought. If you give your hands the freedom to do what they want, they will fidget, which will divert your attention. It is not in a person's natural state to be able to remain motionless for an extended amount of time without using any energy. Whenever you observe someone when they are seated, you will see that they will either move their legs or their hands. Because of your past experiences and your anxious energy, you are used to it. However, when you meditate, you need to be more rooted than that and conscious of what your hands are doing so that they do not become a source of distraction for you. To demonstrate this, bring the tips of your thumb and middle finger together, and if you are seated, rest your hands on the chair's seat in front of you. If you are seated on your cushion, put each hand

on the matching knee with the palms facing upward in this posture. If you are standing, place each hand on the opposite ankle. Because of this, you are much more aware of any movement that you make, and it is far less likely that you will let movement to interfere with your practice of meditation.

The atmosphere of the room
Your option for a room should be one that is pleasant to be in and not too warm. It ought to be a place where you can unwind and take it easy. You shouldn't have anything in the room that may potentially disrupt your concentration on the meditative practice, such as an active computer. When I try to meditate, I do my best work in rooms with walls that are painted in pastel colors. In spite of the fact that I practice meditation with my eyes closed, I still find that noisy wallpapers disrupt the flow of my thoughts. If the room you are meditating in has a distracting wallpaper, turn your

back to it so that the view from your meditative posture is peaceful.

If you want to test how responsive you are going to be or get yourself ready for your meditation, you may just sit in the selected posture and try not to think about anything at all for 10 minutes before you begin. This will give you an idea of how receptive you are going to be. You won't make it through the whole thing, but doing this will help you wind down from your day and release any bad energy that has been building up in your body. Before beginning their first forays into meditation, some individuals practice relaxation techniques, which are simpler forms of the practice. Get into a supine position and shut your eyes. Imagine each individual portion of your body, tighten it up, and then let the tension go. You will be in a better mood for your meditation by the time you have gone head to toe or vice versa, however this is to a significant extent dependent on the amount of time you have given for your session of stretching and breathing exercises. Because a typical session for a novice consists of roughly 20 minutes of meditation, you may wish to complete the relaxation classes first in order to be ready for more in-depth meditation if you have additional time on your hands.

5th Chapter

Just Take It One Step at a Time

The practice of Zen may be done at any time and in any location. If you are experiencing stress, then it is imperative that you take steps toward Zen and relaxation. The majority of today's stress may be attributed to trying to juggle too many tasks at once. The concept of a "multitasker" who is capable of juggling many responsibilities at once is ingrained in the minds of the general population. This is an optical illusion, and studies have shown that individuals are really less productive when they try to do many things at once. People do tasks in the order listed, one at a time, concentrating their whole attention on the activity they are now engaged in. It makes it easier to remember more knowledge, and it also makes it easier to do the work more effectively. Your capacity to concentrate on a single activity to its conclusion without being sidetracked by other concerns will play a significant role in determining whether or not you are successful in pursuing your material goals. When a huge number of individuals start working on a job, what really occurs is that they "get bored" rather than concentrating their attention on the task at hand and doing it successfully. It's possible that these individuals have a lot of fantastic ideas and a lot of projects that they've begun but never finished. Everyone will be able to do far more if they focus on completing one task at a time.

Imagine for a moment that you are a lumberjack armed with a powerful chainsaw. And every 30 seconds, you have to put the chainsaw down in order to answer a message on Whatsapp, SnapChat, or Gmail. This requires you to take your hands off the chainsaw. Your energy would be depleted extremely rapidly and naturally as a result of this.

It would be a lot simpler if you just concentrated on chopping down the tree and responded to all of your messages over lunch. However, the same principle applies to mental labor, such as the creation of eBooks. Imagine you have an assignment to write on Zen Buddhism, but instead of focusing on that, you check your Whatsapp, SnapChat, and Gmail accounts every 30 seconds. When you check these accounts, you also start a dialogue with other individuals who have the same account. However, each time you return to your eBook, you will be required to "pick up" where you left off in the previous reading session. Because it takes the brain some time to go back into its old configuration, it is almost as if you had to abandon all Zen notions in order to have a conversation with friends about a variety of subjects. To put it another way, it requires mental energy. If you aren't careful about who you let message you and when, technology may be a significant drain on your brain capacity. It is really difficult to get any work done when you have many chats happening with multiple people at the same time and are chatting back and forth with each other. This is true in every circumstance. Pay attention to only one thing at a time. Also, be careful about the information that you let settle into your head. Although one's experience of space might be broadened with frequent meditation practice, space itself is not infinite.

It is also important to note that there is no such thing as "multitasking," since this concept does not exist. The human brain, much like a computer, is only capable of concentrating on a single activity at a time, but it can transition between other activities very quickly. Therefore, concentrate your efforts effectively on one job until that work is finished, and then concentrate your efforts effectively on the second task until that task is finished. In the end, it does not make a difference whether you have a million things "to do" or three things "to do." You are only capable of focusing on one activity at a time. It's been said that Zen is both the art of doing one thing at a time and the art of doing nothing at all at the same time.

If we take a more pragmatic approach, one would question how they might improve their capacity to concentrate on one item at a time. There are mainly two different things that need to be done. Your capacity to concentrate will improve dramatically after you eliminate all of the unnecessary information that you've been taking in. This contains everything to do with technology, as well as news and television. People nervously look at their email and other accounts to see whether they have received any alerts. In addition to this, people spend time reading articles that take up space online because they are under the impression that the more they read, the better their life would become. Nevertheless, despite all that is read, very little of it is actually put into practice. Concentration and effort are required for practical application.

The first thing you need to do in order to concentrate your efforts is to watch what you read and pay attention to what you hear. And this is really important: keep track of how much time you spend reading and listening to audiobooks. This also applies to individuals. There is no need to devote any of your time or attention to any individual. It is not in any way unethical to withdraw one's time and attention from those who are squandering one's time. It is your responsibility to offer your time and attention according to the parameters you set.

The second stage in being more focused is to practice the technique of becoming more focused. Set a single goal for yourself. In addition to this, you should not look at any other tasks until the first one has been finished. If you are in the process of writing a book, do not write anything else until you have finished the current project. Don't skimp on the time and effort you put into it. Additionally, while you are doing it, switch off any and all other technological devices. After you have completed writing for the day, make sure this technology is turned back on and respond to any emails that are pertinent. You could also set a goal for yourself to meditate for twenty minutes each day for the following twenty one days. This would be a good alternative. And until you do this assignment, you won't be allowed to read any articles on mindfulness or meditation, nor will you be able to complete any other activities related to mindfulness. This will have a multiplicative effect since meditation also helps you concentrate on things outside of yourself.

Some people claim that they are too busy to accomplish x because they have too many other things on their to-do list. But the primary reason why they have an excessive amount of tasks to do is because they were unable to concentrate on completing one task at a time, therefore they did not finish what they had begun. In a nutshell, if you want to increase your level of productivity, adopting a Zen mindset would need you to do fewer chores but pay closer attention to each one. In addition to that, tackle one activity at a time.

Mindfulness Is About Much More Than Just Stress Relief

The practice of mindfulness often has the effect of lowering levels of stress, although this is not the purpose of the exercise itself. Aware of the inner workings of our mental, emotional, and physical processes is the goal of the practice of mindfulness, which aims to bring one to a state of heightened awareness.

The practice of mindfulness strengthens your body so that it may thrive: Athletes all around the globe practice mindfulness in order to boost their performance and compete at a higher level. From college basketball players practicing acceptance of terrible ideas before games to BMX champions learning to follow their breath and big-wave surfers overcoming their concerns, athletes are finding that mindfulness helps them perform at a higher level. Coach Pete Carroll of the Seattle

Seahawks, along with the assistance of sports psychologist Michael Gervais, discusses teaching the "whole person." A mix of mindfulness, which Gervais refers to as "tactical breathing," and cognitive behavioral training is used by gamers, as shown by the game's designer Hugh Delehanty, to create what Gervais refers to as "full presence and conviction in the moment."

Mindfulness is the source of creative inspiration: Coloring, sketching, and writing are all forms of creative expression that may be accompanied with meditation activities. In addition, we may include mindfulness training into the process of innovation.

The neuronal connections in the brain may be strengthened by mindfulness: We may build new neural pathways and networks in the brain via the practice of mindfulness and other activities that are similar to it. This will improve our ability to focus, as well as our adaptability and awareness. The ability to take care of one's well-being is a skill that may be acquired. Try out this simple meditation to help strengthen the connections in your brain.

A quick glance might help you become a witness to your own thoughts.

In life, we encounter a wide range of nuances and nuances. And if you've ever fought to make sense of a tangle of ideas and felt like you were all alone in that fight, just know that you're not the only one. Aside from that, everyone of us has had this disturbing sensation at some point in our lives, and some of us have had it more often than others. At situations like this, it is difficult to make any choice because there is often uncertainty and confusion that obscure one's ability to exercise solid judgment. What should a character do with themselves? Therefore, the issue that has to be answered is how one may put an end to chaotic ideas and arrive at some level of clarity in their thinking.

Experts on meditation praise the practice for its ability to make such very thing possible for the meditator. Not only does the practice of meditation make it clear that such ideas are vying for one's attention and attempting to cause havoc in one's life, but it also enables the meditator to create a buffer zone between themselves and the commotion and confusion that surrounds them by cultivating the capacity to detach from their experiences and observe them objectively.

Be aware, then, that even in the midst of the cacophony and turmoil, it is this detachment and observation that creates a feeling of calmness in oneself. To put it another way, you develop the ability to step back and take an objective stance, to observe your own ideas without allowing them to dominate or direct you in any way.

The capacity to maintain emotional distance while bearing witness to unfolding events is fundamental to the development of a robust and unclouded intellect. Be conscious of the fact that it does not mean that difficulties, issues, or conflicting and competing demands will evaporate. They won't do that. However, after you have removed yourself from the influence that these kinds of distractions are trying to gain over you, you will be in a better position to choose a course of action.

Getting Started With Meditation — The Actual Practice

When you enter a meditative state, it indicates that you are shifting from one mental and physical state to another as you move through the practice. Imagine you are going through a doorway or a gate. This is the point at which everything will get underway. Before you can pass beyond that threshold, you have to first find a comfortable seat, loosen your muscles, breathe deeply in and out, and bring your mind and body to a state of serenity. After you have finished all of those things, you should start visualizing yourself over the boundary. Now, give this topic of meditation (crossing the threshold) some thought and see if you can bring it into your consciousness.

What are some other topics that you may meditate on?

Symbols and Visual Representations

Having the ability to think in images is not only a helpful talent but also makes visual meditation a lot less difficult. The majority of individuals prefer the notion of meditating or thinking with symbols and images since it helps them develop and bring things to mind. These prompt more in-depth contemplation of more abstract notions and ideals such as love, depth, knowledge, and the passage of time. Some people find that seeing what they need to do helps them recall stuff, organize ideas in their heads, and even put up a timetable.

Thinking using traditional symbols is an effective way to communicate concepts about religion, society, and the afterlife. Consider a candle that has been lit as an illustration. The meanings of hope and tranquility are instantly sent to the person who sits quietly and focuses on a candle that is lit. Some people focus their meditation on moving bodies of water, such as lakes and rivers, which are symbols of ongoing life. Some on rose windows, which are symbolic of the entry of light into several churches.

Taking into consideration the natural world The majority of individuals think that meditating on natural elements, such as waterfalls, the sensation of sand on their feet, the sound of the waves, and even trees and mountains, is very calming. The many symbols that originate from nature are all included in the language that is understood by everyone. Recurring patterns may be seen across the landscape thanks to the natural world. It is analogous to a mountain, which symbolizes fortitude and tenacity; the sun, which stands for a source of life; and waterfalls, which stand for power and creativity, among other things.

Step 2: Delve even farther into your meditation.

As you cross the barrier into step 1, you start your journey into meditation. This is the beginning of your practice. You may see yourself walking through an open door. Now, how about we delve even further? Imagine going through the door to see what's on the other side. You might begin to see a large home with a number of rooms and entrances in it. Imagine that as you continue to go deeper, you are entering door after door, and then all of a sudden you see a stairway and choose to descend it.

A word of advice: try not to hurry things. It is quite OK for you to go slowly but steadily. When you try to picture the scenario in your head, be sure to engage all of your senses. The instant you go through one door, then another door, and then proceed down a flight of stairs, it denotes that you are delving more deeply into your own psyche.

When you have reached the bottom of the staircase, do not rush to climb it just yet; there is still some time until you may do so. You could start exploring, or you could search for a quiet place where you could simply sit down, settle down, and relax. After you have developed this "inner world" via the practice of meditation, you may take use of this skill to enter a deeper level of meditation.

Meditation helps you become more in tune with all of your senses, which may free your creative side. You will become more awake and aware of everything that is going on in your everyday life if you meditate regularly. Fostering one's creative potential may be accomplished through strengthening one's visualization abilities and cultivating one's imagination. As part of the process of becoming more fully yourself, discovering your own unique form of creative expression is essential. Your ability to constructively cope with the many problems that life throws at you will improve if you do so. Keeping an active imagination helps keep your mind sharp, allowing you to get the most out of every session.

Allow your mind's eye to become more open; as you go further into meditation, it is essential that you allow your mind's eye to become more open. What strategy do you plan to use to accomplish this? You make an effort to not only describe the recollections in words, but also to do it via vision. As you think, you can even conjure up detailed visuals in your head. To put this to the test, let's speak the word "water" and see how many different things it brings to mind. Imagine a river or stream with water flowing through it. Now, let the water flow in your hands as you see it doing so in your mind. visualize how satisfying it would be to relieve your thirst as you visualize the water flowing over your skin, how clear it is, and how it feels.

What are some of the other ideas that spring to mind when you think of water? You have to understand that the more you utilize your creative imagination, the more real it will seem to you. Your ability to meditate effectively utilizing "imagery" will improve if you regularly practice using your "mind's eye." During meditation, you will be asked to generate images in your mind's eye. To get the most out of this exercise, let your imagination go wild. You will have the opportunity to use your ideas without any restrictions thanks to this. What strategy do you plan to use to accomplish this? Imagine you are carrying a box that is empty. When you toss this box into the air, the box vanishes from your line of sight. When you look at it, it seems to have bunnies jumping about on it. Keep an eye on them as they jump about you. You extend your hand to grab a rabbit, but it suddenly transforms into a ball before evading your grasp. When you examine the ball in further detail, you will see that an image of a rabbit has been carved inside of it. This is one way in which you might use your creative faculties. It ought to have no boundaries.

What should I do if I find it difficult to concentrate because I am easily distracted? There is no need for alarm. This is to be expected. As you get further into meditation, a large variety of mental distractions will present themselves to you. It is as if you suddenly find that your thoughts are drifting aimlessly and without any prior notice. If you see this happening, do not continue down this path; rather, gently pull yourself back into meditation or into the topic you have chosen to focus on while practicing visualization. At first, it can seem like a bit of a challenge, but eventually, you'll get the feel of it.

In the same manner, if you have trouble seeing something, you might attempt to conjure up a picture in your mind by drawing on all five of your senses. Do not restrict your attention just to the sense of sight or touch. Use all of your senses to their full potential. Because your memory is so rich with memories, it is impossible for you to not have at least one in which you may fully immerse yourself.

Do you remember the smell of the pine trees or the sound of the waves? Experiment with different combinations of the five senses to see which one gives you the greatest confidence.

Look at some of these instances to see what I mean:

The more of your senses you engage, the more potent and vivid the sensations you have on the inside will be. Therefore, do not be scared to test your limits and get familiar with your skills. Who knows, maybe you'll find another ability or talent you never knew you had.

Your sense of touch: when you shut your eyes, can you remember what it's like to run your fingers over the fluffy fur of a dog?

Do you have a strong sense of smell? Can you remember the smell of a newborn from memory?

Sense of taste: Are you able to differentiate between various flavors when you think about them?

Do you have a good ear for music? If you close your eyes and use your imagination, do you think you can hear the sound of an instrument being played?

Sense of sight: Are you able to recollect as much of your past experiences as you possibly can?

The third step is to come out of meditation.

When you have done with your topic, have explored utilizing your imagination, and have arrived at the level of inner peace and tranquility that you were striving for, it is now time to let go of your focus, dissolve the mental images that are now present in your mind, and gradually emerge from the meditative state that you were in. After having crossed the threshold mentally entering the internal world, it is now time to mentally exit the internal world and return to the world outside the threshold. Do not be in a hurry. When you are ready, slowly bring yourself out of the meditative state. Give your body the opportunity to resume its usual breathing pattern. Take your time when you shift your attention to the farthest parts of the planet.

The fourth step is to get ready to rest.

Take some time before going to bed to sit still and think about what happened throughout the day. Consider the events in question as if you were viewing a movie in your head. Attempt to take note of your personal involvement and think back to the events that took place on that day. Try not to focus too much on the things that are going wrong. Do not try to remember the full experience if it was a horrible day and you had a lot of challenges on that particular day. What is the purpose of include this in your meditation practice? Through engaging in this practice, you will be able to cultivate a sense of perspective and continuity that will strengthen every facet of your life. This sort of reflection on one's day is helpful, particularly in situations in which it might be challenging to juggle a variety of duties, obligations, and responsibilities, as well as competing demands from work and the family.

When you attempt to recollect the day without criticizing yourself or the other people in it before you go to sleep, you are turning your thoughts and focusing on yourself instead of other people.

What Exactly Are The Advantages Of Meditating Creatively?

One of the most well recognized advantages of meditation is its ability to lower a person's overall level of stress; but, meditation has many other positive effects as well. Healing occurs on both the physical and mental levels when one meditates.

The following is a short list of the many ways that creative meditation may improve one's overall health and promote a life that is both healthy and happy:

It is well known that practicing creative meditation may help strengthen your immune system. It does this by bolstering the functioning of the neurological system, lowering levels of stress, and activating the parasympathetic nervous system, which is in charge of processes such as "rest and digest," as well as the regeneration and repair of cells.

For the same set of reasons, creative meditation may also help reduce the symptoms of illness by inducing a state of profound relaxation, lowering levels of tension, stress, worry, and anxiety, and contributing to the reduction of pain. In addition to that, it might be of assistance in bringing down elevated blood pressure.

The practice of meditation has been shown to have significant and beneficial effects on a variety of health conditions. It has also been shown that meditation may increase the benefits that one receives from traditional medical therapy. The advice that your physician gives you should never be ignored in favor of your own meditation practice. It is possible for it to supplement, but it cannot take the place of.

Meditation has been shown to be helpful in reducing tiredness and promoting mental attentiveness. It's possible that compared to coffee, it's an even more effective stimulant. For those of you who are unaware, there is a connection between meditating and increasing your level of awareness. That means you can definitely use it if you feel like taking a power nap at your desk at 3 o'clock in the afternoon.

Chronic pain sufferers and the mental anguish they experience as a result may find some respite through the practice of creative meditation.

Meditation not only has good impacts, but it also helps alleviate the symptoms of a number of mental illnesses, including depression, anxiety, and ADD. The mind is trained via the practice of meditation to break rid of destructive thinking patterns.

In addition to these advantages, meditation helps us become less distracted by trivial matters, it teaches us to let go of concerns about the past and the future, it improves our physical health and brings us into more harmony with our inner selves, it fosters greater awareness and innovation, and it sharpens our critical thinking skills.

The practice of creative meditation is also beneficial to the health of the brain. When we become older, the frontal cortex in our brains begins to atrophy and grow thinner. The gray matter in the brain, which is responsible for language, cognition, and the emotional processing, will eventually deteriorate if it is not properly exercised. Because of this degeneration, there is a possibility that our cognitive capacity may continue to deteriorate over time.

The good news is that daily meditation helps to slow down and even reverse the process of brain tissue loss. Meditation is also responsible for thickening sections of the brain that are related with attention and working memory. These are key areas that are linked with intelligence, and meditation thickens these portions of the brain.

Empathy is another skill that may be honed via the practice of creative meditation. Building up our capacity for compassion may have a significant effect on the way we interact with other people. Both forgiving others and having compassion for those who have wronged you are crucial components in developing healthy relationships and a healthy sense of one's own identity. When we have an understanding of the mental and emotional condition of another person, we are better able to put their behaviors into perspective. When you are aware of the pain of other people, you are in a position to take action to relieve that suffering. Compassion has the potential to bring about greater enjoyment for everyone involved. It is undeniably beneficial to the process of loving and accepting oneself.

The question now is, how can we get access to all of these wonderful benefits? In the next chapter, we will discuss the requirements that must be met before you may begin.

How Meditation Helps You Get Rid of Stress (Chapter 2)

The human body is predisposed to respond in some way when it is under stress. Either we choose to run away from what is generating the stress in our lives or we choose to remain and combat it. On the other hand, the consequences might be disastrous if we keep our bodies in a perpetual state of "fight or flight." When one practices meditation, the body goes through the complete reverse of what is described above. The condition of tranquility and a sense of emotional well-being are both enhanced via the practice of meditation. The effects of stress on the body may be reversed via the practice of meditation.

When you first start meditating, you will notice that the tension is being replaced with a sense of tranquility. You will get the sensation that you are once again able to think clearly, and that your mind is not clogged with a thousand different things that are weighing it down. You will notice that you are better equipped to deal with stress when it occurs, and that your responses are different once you have entered that heightened feeling of mental awareness. You will also find that you are able to withstand stressful situations for longer.

Meditation has been shown to reduce the rate of one's heartbeat, raise the degree of happiness one experiences, improve one's ability to sleep, and remove many of the negative side effects and symptoms that are associated with stress. When you meditate, you sharpen your awareness of your mind and engage in much more profound thought. We are able to raise our awareness of stress, how we adjust to that stress and how we react to it, as well as how we worry and the reasons behind our worrying. Once we have achieved the mental state of meditation, we are in a position to change the manner in which we react to worries by putting a non-threatening idea in front of them.

The Methodology Behind Meditating

When you first start meditating, you will experience the following benefits:

Put Your Mind at Ease: When you begin to meditate, your mind will begin to still, and you will notice that the sources of stress in your life begin to go away. Your internal monologue is silent, as it should be, and you shouldn't try to change that. It is far simpler to state something than it is to really carry it through, and doing so will need practice.

A focus on events that occurred yesterday, three weeks ago, or six months ago will only serve to distract you from the here and now. You have no control over the events that will take place tomorrow or in a year from now. You absolutely have to be present in the here and now in order for meditation to work for you. You are only allowed to concentrate on what is happening in the here and now. You have to make the most of each moment, and when it's over, you have to accept that it's over and let it go. Proceed to the next experience that life has to offer, and be sure to enjoy it to the fullest while you still can.

Transform the state of consciousness you are in: You will be able to modify your state of mind and achieve a level of awareness that is midway between being awake and asleep after you have mastered the ability to still the mind and be present in the here and now. When you reach the advanced level of meditation, you will notice a rise in the amount of brain activity in regions associated with happy thoughts and feelings.

www.ingramcontent.com/pod-product-compliance
Lightning Source LLC
Chambersburg PA
CBHW050249120526
44590CB00016B/2273